OCTAVIA ELEMENTARY SCHOOL
UNIT #8
COLFAX, ILLINOIS   61728

P9-DEL-587

B
Jac

E

Mabery, D. L.
This is Michael Jackson

DATE DUE

FEB 1 0 2012			

MEDIALOG
Alexandria, Ky 41001

This Is Michael Jackson

OCTAVIA ELEMENTARY SCHOOL
UNIT #8
COLFAX, ILLINOIS   61728

This Is Michael Jackson

by D.L. Mabery

Lerner Publications Company

Minneapolis

Copyright © 1984 by Lerner Publications Company

All rights reserved. International copyright secured. No part of this book may be reproduced in any form whatsoever without permission in writing from the publisher except for the inclusion of brief quotations in an acknowledged review.

Manufactured in the United States of America

International Standard Book Number: 0-8225-1600-4
Library of Congress Catalog Card Number: 84-10043

1   2   3   4   5   6   7   8   9   10   93   92   91   90   89   88   87   86   85   84

Library of Congress Cataloging in Publication Data

Mabery, D. L.
  This is Michael Jackson.

  Summary: A biography of the young singer/dancer/actor who set a record by winning eight Grammy awards in 1984, becoming the most popular entertainer in the history of the recording business.
  1. Jackson, Michael, 1958-   — Juvenile literature. 2. Afro-American singers — Biography — Juvenile literature. [1. Jackson, Michael, 1958-   . 2. Entertainers. 3. Afro-Americans — Biography]
I. Title.
ML420.J175M3   1984   784.5'4'00924 [B]   84-10043
ISBN 0-8225-1600-4 (lib. bdg.) B_{10}

Contents

The Year of Michael Jackson

Michael Jackson is wearing a brightly colored coat that looks like a navy uniform. He is sitting in the front row at the Grammy Awards, a ceremony to honor the year's best albums and musicians. Michael has already won six awards, and the program is still in progress. Suddenly his name is called again, and he runs back up onto the stage. Michael's album, *E.T. The Extra-Terrestrial,* has been named the best children's recording of the year.

Even though he is indoors, Michael has on
dark glasses. He is also wearing a single glove
on his right hand. The glove is white and
covered with thousands of rhinestones that
sparkle in the lights. Michael receives a trophy
and thanks the audience.

"Of all the awards I've gotten I'm most proud
of this one, honestly," Michael tells everyone at
the ceremony. "Because I think children are a
great inspiration, and this album is not just for
children. It's for everyone. I am so happy and
so proud. And I just want to say thank you
very much."

Before the night is over Michael will once
again make history, this time for winning eight
Grammy awards. In all the years that the
awards have been given out, no one has ever
won that many times. All through the evening,
Michael's dark glasses have covered his eyes.
But when his record *Thriller* wins the award as
Best Album, Michael gives his fans an extra
thrill. He removes his glasses. He explains that
he is doing this for his friend Katharine Hepburn
and for the girls in the balcony, who call out
his name each time he rises to accept
another award.

Onstage at the Grammy Awards with sisters Janet (left) and LaToya, Michael finally takes off his dark glasses.

The Grammys, held early in 1984, marked the end of a year that had seen Michael Jackson become the most popular entertainer in the history of the recording business.   His album *Thriller* was the Number One album on the record charts for most of the year.   The album also contained seven Top Ten singles, "Billie Jean," "Beat It," "The Girl Is Mine," "Human Nature," "Wanna Be Startin' Somethin',"

9

Michael celebrated the world-record-breaking success of his "Thriller" album at a party thrown in his honor by Epic Records.

10

"P.T.Y. (Pretty Young Thing)," and "Thriller."   No other singer has ever managed to do that.   And no other singer has ever sold as many albums as Michael Jackson.

Michael Jackson has captured the love of the whole world with his singing and dancing. When he sang "Billie Jean" on the Motown Special on television, he showed off his latest dance steps.   He spun quickly around on one foot, stopped, pulled up a leg, pulled his jacket open, then spun around quickly again and froze in place.   When the crowd cheered for more, Michael performed a dance step that looks as if he is walking backwards.   That move, the moonwalk, became famous overnight.

Before winning all his awards, Michael reunited with his brothers Jermaine, Jackie, Tito, Marlon, and Randy to record another Jacksons album, *Victory.*   And the brothers started long hours of practicing to get ready for a tour which would take them across the United States during the summer of 1984.

Michael Jackson is loved by millions of people all over the world.   When his hair caught fire from a spark while filming a television commercial for Pepsi, the whole world prayed for him to get well.

Where did this special man come from?

In the Beginning

There was always music in the Jackson household while Michael was growing up. Before Michael was born, his father, Joe, played the guitar in a band called The Falcons. His father later took a job as a crane operator in the steel mills of Gary, Indiana. After the bills were paid, there usually wasn't much left to buy toys for the children. So Katherine, Michael's mother, taught her children to sing the songs she remembered from her own childhood.

"In Gary," said Mr. Jackson, "kids don't have anything to do except go to school and come home." To entertain themselves, the Jackson family sang songs like "Cotton Fields" and "You Are My Sunshine."

Michael Joseph Jackson was born on August 29, 1958. By that time, his oldest sister, Maureen, was already married and living in Kentucky. But the house at 825 Jackson Street was still full of children. In addition to Michael, there were his older sister LaToya and his older brothers, Jackie, Tito, Jermaine, and Marlon. Michael's younger brother, Randy, was born about a year later, and his sister Janet was the baby of the family.

But it was always Michael who was truly special. From the time that he could walk and talk, he would sing and dance around the Jackson house. One day at school, he delighted his kindergarten teachers by singing "Climb Every Mountain" like a true professional.

By this time, three of the Jackson brothers had already formed a singing group. Jermaine sang lead, Jackie sang harmony, and Tito played his father's guitar. When Marlon was six, he started practicing with his brothers. One day the family heard five-year-old Michael imitating Jermaine's voice. Everyone laughed and

OCTAVIA ELEMENTARY SCHOOL
UNIT #8
COLFAX, ILLINOIS   61728

The Jackson Five in 1970: In the back from left to right are Tito, Jackie, and Jermaine. In front are Marlon (left) and Michael.

15

agreed that they had another lead singer.

The five brothers spent most of their free time after school rehearsing. Other kids in the neighborhood teased them because they sang so much. Some of the kids even said things like, "Look at those Jacksons. They won't get anywhere. They are just doing all of that for nothing." It wasn't long before they found out that they were wrong about the Jackson brothers.

Mr. Jackson was proud of his sons' singing group. He helped them practice and taught them new songs. The Jackson Five learned a lot of songs from the records they owned. The first record Michael bought was a song called "Mickey's Monkey" by the Miracles.

The Jackson Five won their first talent show at Roosevelt High School in Gary when Michael was seven years old. Soon the brothers were winning so many talent shows that the living room at 825 Jackson Street was filled with trophies. When the Jackson Five decided to turn professional, they got their first paying job at Mr. Lucky's, a singing club.

"When we sang," said Michael, "people would always throw all this money on the floor. Tons of dollars and lots of change. I remember my pockets being so full of money that I couldn't keep my pants up!"

As the Jackson Five became more popular, the group drove to other cities to perform. "Let's go, boys," Mr. Jackson would say. The brothers would climb into the family Volkswagen bus and do their homework on the trip. They knew they had to keep their grades up, whether or not they performed every night. If one of them fell behind in school, that brother had to stay home. The Jackson Five worked very hard. Many times they would have to ride all night to return home from a concert. The next morning they still had to go to school.

At a concert in their hometown, Diana Ross saw the Jackson Five perform. Diana was already a famous star and had several records on the Motown label. She was so impressed with the boys that she immediately called Berry Gordy, head of her record company, and told him what she saw.

Berry Gordy arranged a party at his home in Detroit and asked the Jackson Five to sing. After their show, everyone at the party stood up and cheered. Berry Gordy came over and shook their hands. Not long after that, the Jackson Five were offered a chance to make records for Motown.

After the brothers landed their job with

In 1971 the Jackson Five made a guest appearance on the Sonny & Cher Comedy Hour.

Motown Records, the family moved from Gary to Los Angeles, California, where the offices of Motown Records are located. Half of the group, including Michael, lived with Diana Ross. The other half stayed with Berry Gordy. They didn't return to Gary for two years.

"I lived with Diana for almost a year and a half," recalls Michael. "It was like paradise. We went to Disneyland and had fun every day."

Before the Jackson Five made their first record, they learned a lot about show business.

The Jackson Five in 1972: From left to right are Tito, Marlon, Jackie, Michael, and Jermaine.

The boys took special classes to learn how to dance and how to talk on television. Even then Michael's teachers could tell that he was a talented dancer. After a year of studying, the Jackson Five went into the recording studio to make their first record.

To make sure that a record sounds right, record companies use producers. The producer works with the performers and hires the musicians who will back them up. In this way, the producer helps to shape the sound that you

19

hear when you play a record.

The Jackson Five had not one but several producers. This group of men became known as "The Corporation." The Corporation produced the Jackson Five and also wrote songs for the group. These were new songs that no one else had recorded. With the help of The Corporation, the Jackson Five recorded "I Want You Back," which Motown released as their first single.

In the fall of 1969, The Jackson Five appeared with Diana Ross on the television show "The Hollywood Palace." The first song they sang was a ballad called "Can You Remember." After the applause, Michael looked right into the camera and said, "Now we'd like to do our very first release on Motown. It's on sale everywhere!" The boys sang "I Want You Back" and danced around the stage with incredible energy. The crowed cheered wildly when the song was finished.

That was the night that the Jackson Five became big stars. Jackie was 18 years old, Tito was 16, Jermaine was 15, Marlon was 12, and Michael was only 11 years old! "I Want You Back" was so popular when it came out that it became the Number One record in America.

The Jackson Five recorded more songs that

became Number One hits. Their fans pushed "ABC," "I'll Be There," and "Never Can Say Goodbye" to the top of the charts. Soon the Jackson Five had sold more records than anyone else on Motown Records. Even as a young boy, Michael Jackson was making history.

The Jackson Five won even more awards, too. When a group sells 500,000 records in the United States, they win a Gold Record. If they sell one million records they get a Platinum Record. The Jackson Five became so popular that there is now a special room in their California house for all their gold and platinum records.

But one of the most special awards came to the Jacksons on January 31, 1971. The family returned to Gary, Indiana, to perform two special concerts. It was the Jacksons' first time back in their hometown since they had become famous recording stars. Even though there was a huge snow storm that day, thousands of fans were waiting to greet the helicopter that brought the group to West Side High School.

At the Gary City Hall, the mayor presented the Jackson Five with the key to the city. When they drove by their old house at 825 Jackson Street, there was a large sign hanging from the roof that said WELCOME HOME JACKSON FIVE.

Michael On His Own

The first record Michael Jackson appeared on alone was the single "Got To Be There." This record was released when Michael was 12 years old. It became an immediate success. This song also went to Number One on the record charts, and Michael became even more popular. Even though it looked like Michael would become a very big singing artist without his brothers, he still recorded albums with the Jackson Five.

Many people wonder if Michael's brothers might feel left out because of all the attention he gets. "I've been doing this since I was five years old onstage and I feel it's something that God gave me to do," Michael says. "I'm the one who sings lead. They can sing lead, but I've been chosen to sing lead on the songs, and I'm thankful to be chosen. They kind of understand it, and they accept it because that's what I do."

Mrs. Jackson feels that she raised her sons in a home where they received a lot of love and attention, and they are not jealous about Michael's success. "We used to talk to the boys about getting big heads," she said. "None of them is better than anyone else. One might have a little more talent, but that doesn't make you better. You're just the same as anyone else. It's just a job. Other people might be doctors and lawyers, but Michael entertains because maybe that's what he can do best. That doesn't mean he's better."

A year after Michael's first solo record, he released another single that became the best-selling song for Motown Records in 10 years. It was a beautiful ballad telling the story of a trusting friendship between a boy and a pet rat. The song "Ben" won Michael another Gold Record award.

Michael played the part of the scarecrow and Diana Ross was Dorothy in the movie version of *The Wiz,* which came out in 1977.

"I love rats, you know, like Ben," Michael said. "I really do feel like I'm talking to a friend when I play with them."

The song "Ben" came from a movie about a boy who raised rats. Though Michael did not act in that movie, this was the first time he became involved with films. His opportunity to act came later when he played the part of the scarecrow in the movie *The Wiz.*

Acting has always been one of Michael's dreams. "I love acting so much," he says. "It's fun. What is wonderful about film is that you can become another person."

The Wiz was made using the same story from another movie called *The Wizard of Oz*. *The Wiz* was different because all the actors and dancers in it were black. Michael's longtime friend Diana Ross also starred in the movie. While working on the movie in New York City, Michael met a man named Quincy Jones. Quincy Jones was producing the music for *The Wiz*. He would later become Michael's producer for the albums *Off the Wall* and *Thriller*.

The Wiz did not become a big hit movie, but Michael learned a lot about performing in front of a movie camera. Later when Michael made the videos for the songs from his *Thriller* album, this movie training came in handy.

Shortly before filming for *The Wiz* began, the Jackson Five decided to leave Motown Records for a different record company. They chose Epic Records. While working for Motown Records, the Jackson Five had become famous stars. The men known as The Corporation always wrote the songs for the Jackson Five and always produced the records.

By now Michael and his brothers Jermaine, Tito, and Jackie were beginning to write their own songs, and they wanted to record them. Motown wanted them to sing The Corporation's songs. The Jackson Five also wanted to try to produce their own records instead of having The Corporation do the job.

Jermaine, Michael's older brother, had married Berry Gordy's daughter Hazel. Since Berry Gordy was the head of Motown Records, Jermaine was torn between staying with Motown Records and going with his brothers to Epic Records. He finally decided to stay with Motown.

Without Jermaine, the Jackson Five now became known as The Jacksons. At Epic, The Jacksons started writing and producing their own songs.

Even though it was fun for Michael to sing his own songs, things seemed different to him. "Ever since we started singing, Jermaine was in a certain spot near me onstage," said Michael. "All of a sudden he was gone. It felt bare on that side for a long time."

When Michael Jackson was 22 years old, he again went into the recording studio to make a record without his brothers. The album was called *Off The Wall,* and four of the singles went

Michael and Diana each received an American Music Award in 1981 — Michael for his album "Off the Wall" and Diana for her single "Upside Down."

straight to the top of the charts. Once again Michael made history, since no solo artist had ever had four hit singles on one album before. *Off The Wall* sold more copies than anyone had ever planned, and Michael received a platinum award for this record too.

Now Michael Jackson was a real superstar, and he started to do a lot of other projects. He wrote and produced the song "Muscles" for his friend Diana Ross. And he learned a lot more about acting from another friend, Jane Fonda.

In 1983, good friends Michael and Jane Fonda shared each other's excitement when both received platinum album awards, Michael for "Thriller" and Jane for "Jane Fonda's Workout Record."

Michael had met Jane Fonda at a party in Hollywood. When she was working on the movie *On Golden Pond,* she invited Michael to come and visit her. On location, Michael watched Jane Fonda and the other actors make the movie. At night he would sit and talk with Jane about acting, history, and different countries of the world. Katharine Hepburn and Henry Fonda, Jane's co-stars in the movie, also talked to Michael about acting. And Henry Fonda taught Michael how to fish.

29

Quincy Jones received a Grammy for his work on "Thriller."

When Michael returned to California, he started to work on his next album, *Thriller*. With the help of his producer, Quincy Jones, Michael chose the songs and the musicians he wanted for the record.   He wanted the music to send a message to all people, whether they were black or white.   That message was to be happy.   Michael got his message across in a big

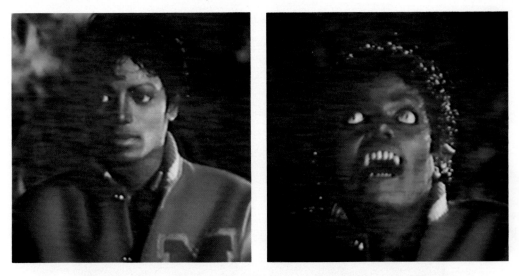

"I'm not like other guys," warns Michael in his "Thriller" video.

way. *Thriller* is the most popular album in history and has sold over 33 million copies around the world.

For three of the songs that Michael sang on *Thriller*, Michael filmed videos to be shown on the MTV cable television channel. By now most of you have seen these videos on television.

The two most popular videos are "Beat It" and "Thriller." The "Thriller" video is a small monster movie. In it Michael turns into a werewolf and later dances in the street with a whole neighborhood of ghouls. At the end viewers find out that it was all a dream.

31

The "Beat It" video created a whole new dancing style.

When Michael filmed "Beat It," he used real street gang members along with professional dancers for the knife-fight scene.

In "Beat It," Michael stops two street gangs from a knife fight. Instead of fighting, the kids end up dancing to Michael's song. With his usual style, Michael uses music and magic to turn hate into love.

Michael at Home

When Michael Jackson isn't working,
you won't find him at the beach or driving his car
around the streets of Los Angeles. Michael
spends most of his time at home where he feels
comfortable. Even though he grew up
performing onstage, Michael is really very shy.
When he is not doing concerts, he stays home
writing songs, drawing cartoons, or talking with
his friends on the phone. Sometimes he will
ride around the yard in a little electric car, the
same kind used at Mr. Toad's Wild Ride
in Disneyland.

Onstage, Michael will dance and spin and kick his legs up high while singing. But when he is not performing, he doesn't go to many parties. He is far too shy to speak to someone he has never met.

Part of the reason Michael is so shy is that he didn't live the way most kids do. When he was young, he was so busy practicing and performing that he missed out on a lot of the things most people do to have fun. Michael cannot remember ever going trick-or-treating on Halloween, and he never had a school chum or playmate to ride bicycles with.

"I hate to admit it, but I feel strange around everyday people," Michael has said. "See, my whole life has been on stage. And the impression I get of people is applause, standing ovations and them running after you."

This is why Michael enjoys giving concerts. "Onstage is the only time I really open up. I say to myself, this is it. This is home. This is where I'm supposed to be, where God meant me to be. Performing is better than anything else I can think of!"

Because Michael is seen on television and in concerts so much, most people he meets do not treat him like a next-door neighbor. If he goes out to see a movie, he will always be approached by people wanting to take his picture or touch him just to make sure he is really there.

When Michael wants to get away from his work, he sometimes rides his bike over to a schoolyard to be with the children playing there. Michael feels that children are very special, and he likes to talk to them and learn from them.

Michael also loves animals. In back of his house is his own private zoo. He owns four swans, two that are black and two that are white. He had a pond built in the backyard so that his swans have a place to swim. Next to the pond are large bird cages surrounded by trees. Here he keeps wild birds, including parrots and peacocks. He has two deer and a ram that he calls Mr. Tibbs, and he lets them all run free in the yard.

One of Michael's most unusual pets is a llama. Llamas live in the mountains of South America and have wool like sheep. Michael bought his llama from a traveling circus. His name is Louis, and he can perform tricks like walking on his knees.

Inside the house in Michael's bedroom is still another pet. This one is an eight-foot-long snake, a boa constrictor named Muscles. Most people are afraid of snakes, but not Michael. He

Two of Michael's closest friends are Muscles...

says that snakes are very misunderstood and that they can be very gentle.

Michael loves animals so much that he has chosen to be a vegetarian.   He eats no meat at all.   He drinks a lot of fruit juices and eats vegetables, fruits, and nuts.   Each Sunday he fasts, or goes without eating, for the full day.   People who fast do so to clean out their bodies.

. . .and Louis.

Michael lives in a large house in Encino, California, a town where a lot of other singers and movie stars live. For years his whole family lived there. When his brothers married and moved into their own houses, Michael had the house redesigned. Now he lives there with his parents and two sisters, LaToya and Janet. "If I moved out, I'd die of loneliness," Michael has said.

Michael's magic kingdom has an old-fashioned popcorn machine in the courtyard, a swimming pool, and a pond for his swans, all surrounded by well-kept gardens and a brick wall.

Michael designed the house to be like a little magic kingdom.   There are rooms in the house where Michael can practice dancing for hours without stopping.   In one room, Michael has video games like Frogger, Space Invaders, and Pac-Man so he can play them whenever he wants.   Michael also has a large collection of cartoons and a small movie theater in which to watch them.

Next to the living room is an old-fashioned soda fountain where Michael serves his guests ice cream, milkshakes, and sodas.   The most unusual room in Michael's magic kingdom, though, will be full of robots dressed as pirates.   It is being built by the same people who helped build Disneyland, and will look like the Disneyland ride "Pirates of the Caribbean."

Disneyland is, in fact, Michael's favorite place in the world.   When he is not on tour, he visits Disneyland and Walt Disney World in Florida every chance he can.   At the Hotel Royal Plaza in Orlando, he can even stay in "The Michael Jackson Room," which was named especially for him.

Tomorrow

No one really knows what Michael Jackson will do next. He has already made history so many times, and it is certain that any new records he makes will bring him even more awards. Michael has talked about making a movie based on one of his favorite books, *Peter Pan,* but so far no firm plans have been announced.

Michael Jackson is a person with many talents. We can be sure that whatever he does, whether he sings, dances, or acts in movies, it will have that special magic that can only come from Michael Jackson.

Records and Awards

Michael Jackson's Musical History

Singles

Motown

** **I Want You Back**   1969, #**1**

** **ABC**   1970, #**1**

** **The Love You Save / Found That Girl**   1970, #**1**

** **I'll Be There**   1970, #**1**

* **Mama's Pearl**   1971, #**1**

* **Got To Be There**   1971, Solo, #**1**

* **Rockin' Robin**   1971, Solo

* **Never Can Say Goodbye**   1971

Maybe Tomorrow   1971

* **Sugar Daddy**   1971

Little Bitty Pretty One   1972

I Wanna Be Where You Are   1972, Solo

Lookin' Through the Windows   1972

** **Ben**   1972, Solo, #**1**

* **Corner of the Sky**   1972

With a Child's Heart   1973, Solo

Hallelujah Day   1973

Get It Together   1973

**   **Dancin' Machine** 1974

What Ever You Got, I Want 1974

I Am Love (Part I & II) 1975

Forever Came Today 1975

We're Almost There 1975, Solo

Just a Little Bit of You 1975, Solo

Epic

*   **Enjoy Yourself** 1976

Show You the Way To Go 1977

Goin' Places 1977

Ease on Down the Road (with Diana Ross, From *The Wiz,* on MCA Records) 1978

Blame It on the Boogie 1978

You Can't Win (Part I) 1979, Solo

**   **Shake Your Body Down to the Ground** 1979

**   **Don't Stop 'til You Get Enough** 1979, Solo, **#1**

* **Rock with You** 1979, Solo, **#1**

* **She's Out of My Life** 1980, Solo

Lovely One 1980

Heartbreak Hotel 1980

Can You Feel It 1981

Walk Right Now 1981

* **The Girl Is Mine** (with Paul McCartney) 1982

* **Billie Jean** 1983, Solo, **#1**

* **Beat It** 1983, Solo, **#1**

* **Wanna Be Startin' Something** 1983, Solo

Human Nature 1983, Solo

P.Y.T. (Pretty Young Thing) 1983, Solo

45

** **Say Say Say** (with Paul McCartney)   1983, **#1**

Thriller   1983, Solo

Guest Appearances:
Somebody's Watching Me by Rockwell (Motown, 1984)

Tell Me I'm Not Dreamin' (Too Good to Be True) by Jermaine Jackson (Arista, 1984)

Albums

Motown

* **Diana Ross Presents The Jackson Five**   1969
* **ABC**   1970

Third Album   1970

* **Christmas Album**   1970

Maybe Tomorrow   1971

* **TV Soundtrack: Goin' Back to Indiana**   1971
* **Jackson 5 Greatest Hits**   1972

Got To Be There   1972, Solo

* **Ben**   1972, Solo
* **Lookin' Through the Windows**   1972

Get It Together   1973

* **Dancing Machine**   1974

Forever, Michael   1975, Solo

Best of Michael Jackson   1975, Solo

Joyful Jukebox Music   1975

* **The Jackson Five Anthology Album**   1976

One Day in Your Life   1978, Solo

Epic

  *   **The Jacksons** 1976

     Goin' Places 1977

** **Destiny** 1978

** **Off the Wall** 1978, Solo

     Triumph 1981

     The Jacksons Live (2-record set) 1981

     E.T.: The Extra-Terrestrial Storybook MCA Records, 1982

** **Thriller** 1982, Solo

  *   Gold Record

** Platinum Record

#1 Number One Record

Grammy Awards

ABC Single, Best Pop Song, 1971

Don't Stop 'til You Get Enough Single, Best Male R & B Vocal, 1979

Thriller Album of the Year, 1983

Beat It Single, Record of the Year, 1983

(**Thriller** also won six other Grammys for its producers and songwriters in 1983)

47

Photo Credits

Henry Diltz: p. 12
Sam Emerson/California Features: pp. 38, 39
Epic Records: p. 42
Photo Features International: pp. 1, 19, 32, 33, 34, 40
Photoreporters: Phil Roach, p. 2; James Colburn, pp. 10, 31;
    Jim McCrary, p. 22
Wide World Photos: pp. 6, 9, 15, 18, 25, 28, 29, 30
Front Cover: Chris Walter/Photo Features International
Back Cover: James Colburn/Photoreporters